C000110050

Dominic Barberi

by
Fr Ben Lodge, C.P.

*All booklets are published thanks to the
generous support of the members of the
Catholic Truth Society*

CATHOLIC TRUTH SOCIETY
PUBLISHERS TO THE HOLY SEE

Contents

A Rich Legacy

"My dear Sisters, without face you cannot be shaved!" This would appear to be an interesting opening for a Retreat priest addressing a group of Religious Sisters. However, this is only one of many stories told of the Italian Priest who never quite mastered the pronunciation of English. In fact he was trying to tell them an equally profound truth: "Without faith you cannot be saved." In a similar way while visiting the Convent of Mercy in Handsworth he heard how the Sisters were instructing many male converts, but a number of Sisters were developing scruples. He said to them "My dear Sisters, I believe you are making many converts and that many of them are men. That is good. I am told some of the Sisters have a scruple about instructing men. Have no fear Sisters. You are all too old and too ugly."

Saints

Saints are people rooted in their time and culture, who often challenge the values of their day. If they were alive today they would face similar challenges but in different circumstances. For while time marches on, and history is said to advance, there is little to suggest that the human spirit changes or develops from generation to generation. The conflicts between good and evil, rich and poor, powerful and powerless remain. Central to all of this is an individual's relationship with God.

Over the centuries the Church has examined the lives of a number of individuals, and having found their lives to be exemplary, and even inspirational, have held them up to be admired by the whole Church, by declaring them to be saints, i.e. people whose lives are worthy of imitation. Usually a saint would be admired for one specific virtue e.g. Francis for his poverty, Maria Goretti for her purity, Oscar Romero for his fight for social justice etc.

Each century appears to produce characters who can be admired as inspirational in the era in which they lived, and even leave a lasting legacy to influence not only the Church but the wider world. We think of people like St Augustine, St Benedict, St Francis, St Teresa and St Ignatius. Others may not enjoy an international cult of celebrity, but nonetheless they have exerted a profound influence in a particular area of the Church. One such man was Dominic Barberi (1792-1849), an Italian Religious priest who was totally committed to the conversion of England, and was instrumental in establishing ecumenical dialogue.

Back in 1926 Cardinal Francis Bourne wrote of Dominic: "Of all the preachers of the divine Word who have worked for the salvation of souls in England, there is no one, in our opinion, to whom we are more indebted than the Servant of God, Dominic of the Mother of God... I should consider myself happy if I had the power and right to dedicate this whole Diocese to his care and protection, and be allowed to honour him as our Patron and Protector in England. His story is another proof of the special love which our Divine Master has for England."

A prophet in his time

The Second Vatican Council closed on 8th December 1965, having concentrated on its declared twin purposes of bringing about pastoral renewal and fostering unity between the Catholic Church and her separated brethren, in other words promoting Christian Unity. These were the ideals of Dominic Barberi.

On 27th October 1963 Pope Paul VI said: "Blessed Dominic's beatification brings to light a character who has more than one claim to outstanding merit... He is worthy of remembrance as a scholastic author of sound studies in theology and philosophy. His work on papal infallibility, for example, anticipates the definition which was to be made many years later by the [First] Vatican Council."

The late Pope John Paul II had tremendous devotion to Our Lady (someone to be imitated for her total faith in God), and so the Pope incorporated the letter "M" into his coat of arms. His successor Benedict XVI, in his inaugural speech, declared his intention to work for

Christian Unity. In the light of these recent events, it would appear that this is an appropriate time to make more widely known, the life of a man whose whole life was dedicated to Mary as he worked to develop the movement for Christian Unity: Dominic Barberi.

Dominic was an apostle of ecumenism in days when ecumenism was virtually unheard of. He has often been referred to in little more than a footnote explaining that he was the priest who received John Henry Newman into the Catholic Church. The truth is far greater, and his story is such as to render his reception of Newman as little more than one small episode in his own heroic life. This heroism was recognised when Dominic was declared Blessed in 1963.

What Dominic would make of his Cause for canonisation must remain a moot point; however, the nuns of Colwich Abbey in Staffordshire recorded at the time of one of his retreats to them, that he said "We must all be saints, though not canonised ones; it is too expensive!"

Early Life

Dominic Barberi was born at Pallanzana, a hamlet not far from Viterbo, about fifty miles north of Rome, in the Papal States, on 22nd June 1792, one year after the passing of the "Relief Act" in England, by which Catholics were once more allowed to practise their religion openly, after three centuries of persecution. Two days after his birth Dominic was taken to the local church and baptised by the Carmelite parish priest.

The world into which Dominic was born was a troubled one. The French Revolution of 1789 had shaken France, and with it Europe, to their social foundations. This was to prepare the ground for Napoleon's invasion of Italy in 1796.

Childhood

Dominic's parents had eight children, five boys and three girls. Dominic, being the youngest and his mother's favourite, was not saved from being chastised. When any of the children did misbehave, she would say "children you can be saints". This was a phrase Dominic subsequently encouraged other parents to use with their children!

Contemporaries comment that while the family had very little materially, the children were brought up in "the fear and love of God", and in the faithful practice of their religious duties. The children were taught not only by instruction, but also by the virtuous example of their parents. During his novitiate Dominic recalled how his mother would return home from the mill with an empty sack - having given the flour away to those in greater need.

However, Maria Barberi was perceptive and quickly realised that her youngest son was talented. She could see that he was lively, intelligent and extremely affectionate. She also realised that when she made a fuss of him, he encouraged her artfully by feigning indifference; apparently she allowed this subterfuge to continue.

Central to the spirituality of the mother, which was handed on to the children, was an absolute trust in the Providence of God. This did not lead to some miserable state of life, but rather to a great sense of joy. Dominic often quoted one of her sayings: "a hundred years of gloom do not pay off a farthing of debt." In later life Dominic would frequently take as a theme the patience of a mother, no doubt inspired by his own mother. And yet Maria his mother had always insisted to all her children that Mary, their heavenly Mother, loved them immensely more than she did. As a matter of course, the family would fast on every Saturday and on the vigils of Our Lady's feasts.

His father died when Dominic was three, and things looked grim. Maria, his mother, broke her arm and was taken to hospital where she was told that it would be several weeks before she could return home to look after her children. Maria invoked the help of the Blessed Virgin with such confidence that she was cured immediately, and so went home to her family.

Education

As far as education was concerned, Dominic received instruction in the rudiments of letters from the local Capuchin community. From the age of three, whenever he met anyone who could read, he produced a book and asked them to help him. His very limited education was not because of lack of schools or teachers, and even less because of a lack of talent on Dominic's part, but due to the simple way of living in the family. He himself reports that when he was six or seven years old he was sent to the Capuchins of Pallanzana who had the charity to teach him, but this was constantly interrupted for a variety of reasons. He would arrive and find his teacher too busy to spend time with him, and so would return home crying with the disappointment.

While the family was not poverty stricken, they were respectable and independent tenant farmers, his parents, and later his uncle-farmer could see little point in Dominic going to school if he was going to work in the fields. In appearance Dominic was short and stocky, and every inch a peasant. He had high cheek-bones, but the feature which most people noticed was his lively, laughing, piercing dark eyes. From the earliest days it became obvious that Dominic had a phenomenal memory. He learned to read the Scriptures, and learned whole sections by heart, apparently without too much effort. Possibly the most celebrated story to illustrate the power of his memory was told by a later companion of Dominic, Fr Gaudentius Rossi CP. He reports that Dominic read for the first time seventy long verses of Tasso's *Gerusalemme Liberata*, he shut the book and recited them all from beginning to end! In a similar way he was able to repeat sermons which he had heard at the parish church almost word for word. Clearly Dominic had an exceptional memory which was married to a sharp intellect, but his prodigious memory caused a few people to believe that his knowledge of Latin had been acquired supernaturally - something he was very quick to deny.

Confirmation

At the age of seven Dominic was Confirmed in the Bishop of Viterbo's chapel on 9th June 1799. His first Communion was made five years later when he was twelve. Dominic was devoted to reciting the Rosary on a daily basis, and he made frequent use of the sacraments. As his reading ability improved, he started to read the lives of the saints. He found an old Latin Bible in his uncle's house, and with the help of a dictionary began to understand the Scriptures. Subsequently he recalled "I had an intense longing to study...when I met anyone who could read, I got him to teach me." Thirst for knowledge remained a passion for the rest of his life.

Family

Dominic was very fond of his sister Rose, who was one year older. He told the story of how one day they were sent by their mother to collect some water in a glass jug from a nearby fountain. The jug got broken and Dominic began to cry, fearing punishment when he got home. Shrewdly Rose instructed him to stop crying and to save his tears until they would meet their mother. She reasoned that if they both started to cry when they met their mother she would assume something terrible had happened, and in fact would be relieved to discover that it was only the jug which had been broken, and so would forget to scold the children. The strategy worked, and when they explained about the broken jug she said "Is that all?" and gave them a plate of sweets to stop their tears.

The fact that the family was steeped in a sense of the presence of God can best be illustrated by a story told by Dominic. He explained that in Italy when a child dies, those of a similar age attend the funeral with the girls wearing veils and crowns of roses on their heads. One day Rose had been attending such a funeral. When she came home she told her brother that when she died, she would like to be dressed in the same manner as the little girl just buried, and to have beautiful white roses all over her. Her eldest sister overheard this and said she would take care of all that when Rose was dead.

Tired after the funeral, Rose went to bed where she collapsed and died suddenly. The mother was out of the house and Dominic was the only witness to her death. However, he was not upset but envious as he felt that Rose had got to heaven first. As soon as his mother appeared on her way home, Dominic ran out to meet her and announced "Mamma, Rose is dead." She almost collapsed with the shock, but Dominic persisted "Why Mamma, isn't Rose lucky to have gone to heaven so soon?"

Talent

As a child with a pleasant nature and quick mind, Dominic soon established himself as a favourite not only in the family circle, but in the surrounding hamlets. As the "scholar of the village" he used to delight the local peasants by telling them stories from the Middle Ages. His lack of formal education did not impact on his human or emotional development. No doubt his prodigious memory stood him in good stead.

The point is that Dominic had tremendous natural talent and should never be written off as "a peasant" without any intellectual ability - something Newman was to acknowledge years later. Dominic was intellectually gifted well above the average, and when this gift was married to his thirst for knowledge he was able to grow in his enthusiasm for study. This was to prove to be the foundation for his future missionary activity and his life's endeavour, working for the conversion of England.

From an early age Dominic spent much of his time in the country where he was able to observe nature and be open to the movement of God in his life. In his autobiography he wrote: "I recall my God that almost as soon as I came to the use of reason, you made yourself known to me in a mysterious way... You permitted me to hear you whispering in my ear 'Love me my son.'" Dominic soon learned to put his trust in God - and he was never disappointed.

Spiritual formation

It would appear that Maria Barberi knew her death was rapidly approaching, and true to her trust in the Providence of God, she happily set about preparing for death, to the point of sewing her own shroud. In 1803 Maria died and Dominic, aged eleven, moved onto his uncle's farm at Merlano near Viterbo where they cultivated vines, olives and chestnuts. This was not an easy transition for he felt totally abandoned, despite his uncle treating him like his own son. He subsequently wrote that he turned to Mary and said "you inspired me with greater confidence than ever in your maternal protection. I recall that day when I was orphaned and felt like one derelict and abandoned in an unknown continent. I had recourse to you, and only dimly aware of what I said, exclaimed "O! Most holy Virgin, you see my plight. You see that I am deprived of a mother on earth, so now it is up to you to be my Mother. To you I commit myself, in you I trust, from today you shall be my Mother." The subsequent life of Dominic proves that Mary accepted her new role.

The faith taught to him by his late mother Maria gradually weakened, and Dominic concluded that it was quite fair that Popes Pius VI and VII should be punished and humiliated by deportation for opposing Napoleon, the so-called liberator of Italy. No doubt the wave of atheistic literature which flooded Europe after the French Revolution had a major impact on Dominic. His uncle and aunt were in no position to examine and guide the literature the young man was exposed to.

As Dominic's uncle took no interest in any intellectual formation, the literature Dominic eventually immersed himself in was often atheistic and subversive. Though he never renounced his faith, he allowed cynical and sceptical thoughts to dominate his thinking for some time. He later wrote "Piety seemed to me despicable, and the only men worth calling great, those who had enlightened the world by arms or literary work. I considered the Christian religion mean and contemptible, and the world debased by having become Christian."

Questionings

He continued to frequent the Sacraments, say his Rosary and formal prayers, but for much of the time Dominic was a dreamer, a Romantic. In his fantasy he created his ideal lover, but this was rapidly replaced when he fell in love with the sister of a friend; a friend who was chosen because of his sister! The first problem was that the girl was already engaged, and Dominic never tried to change that. However, he took great delight in fancying himself in love with her, and in entertaining gallant thoughts about her. He gave up the practice of mental prayer, but continued to pray the Rosary. Writing about this period in his life he stated that giving her up made his joints creak and "I felt that as long as she was with me, I could have been happy, even in hell." His love was pure and idyllic, and when the girl eventually married he felt a sense of relief and liberation.

Despite his apparent lapses in religious fervour, Dominic, according to one of the Benedictine nuns at Colwich, discovered that "God communicated to him. For a notable time, a supernatural light, and that from that time onward (1806), there was implanted in his soul an extraordinary thirst for the salvation of souls, particularly for the conversion of unbelievers, for whom he prayed continually."

Religious contacts

Not far from Merlano the Passionists had established a Retreat at Vetralla, twenty-five miles to the northeast of Civitavecchia, and Dominic must have been aware of it as a child. The Passionists had been founded in Italy by St Paul of the Cross (1694-1775) as a missionary Order to give parish missions and to give retreats, hence their communities are referred to as Retreats. The Rule of the Order was very strict and severe, with a great emphasis on poverty. The way of life for a Passionist was clearly laid down as one of being immersed in meditating on the Passion of Christ, and then spending no more than half of each year out on apostolic work preaching missions or giving retreats; the other half of the year was to be spent in prayer at the foot of the cross. The purpose of this was not only to draw closer to Christ, but to be able to serve all in society, especially the poorest of the poor. The work of the Passionist is firmly rooted in their motto "We preach Christ Crucified." This was not some negative or painful view of the Passion, but rather saw the Passion as the greatest love story ever told. Paul of the Cross had longed for the conversion of England and dreamed of sending Passionists not only there, but to the surrounding countries of northern Europe.

The Religious Orders had been suppressed by Napoleon, and the Passionists were forced to leave

Vetralla. They moved into a house just a short distance from Dominic in Merlano. Each morning Dominic would serve Mass for the priests in their chapel, and he was given free access to their library. Once while walking in Viterbo he saw a Passionist walking in his black habit and wearing the Passionist sign of a white heart surmounted by a cross. We are told that "a mighty love and attraction for our Congregation took hold of him, and at the same moment, an innermost conviction that one day he too would wear the badge of the Passionist." Humanly speaking, this must have seemed an impossible dream to Dominic, not least because his uncle and the local parish priest were developing plans to appoint Dominic as heir to the uncle's property, and to arrange his marriage with a young woman of the neighbourhood.

Marriage prospects

His uncle became insistent that the marriage to the unnamed girl should take place, but there was a problem. In a moment of fervour Dominic had made a vow to give himself wholly to God by entering the Congregation of the Passion. Without seeking advice from any of the Passionists, he went and found an unknown priest and explained his predicament; the priest, after carefully listening, sided with the uncle. After a prolonged struggle Dominic finally decided to ignore his vow and to enter into marriage. However, on the day he was to be married he fell dangerously ill with a violent fever and received the last rites of the Church.

As he lay at the point of death, he saw himself in a vision before the court of God, weighed down with the guilt of his broken vow. Demons were around him waiting to carry him off when sentence would be passed. But Mary, his heavenly mother did not forget him. She interceded with her Son for the soul of Dominic Barberi, and promised that the vow would be kept, and that he would work for the greater glory of God while life should last. The crisis passed. Dominic recovered, wavered again, and finally committed himself to the Passionists.

Conscription

At the same time as Dominic struggled with the prospect of getting married, another crisis fell upon him. Napoleon, planning to invade Russia, had to increase the size of his army and so introduced a form of conscription in the Papal States. These were the parts of Italy which acknowledged the temporal sovereignty of the Papacy; by 1870 all that remained of them was Vatican City. Dominic certainly did not want to be in the army of an Emperor who had proved to be such an opponent to the Church, and in particular the Popes. Dominic's name was on the ballot paper and each name was allocated a number. He had a dream in which his mother told him that he would be exempt from conscription; she advised him to join the Confraternity of the Holy Rosary. He immediately went and enrolled, and increased his prayers and works of piety. When the day came for the drawing of numbers, Dominic drew a very high number and so he escaped conscription. Of the forty thousand young men who left the Papal States, only two thousand returned. The 1812 campaign to Moscow had been a disaster.

Passionist fathers

At about the age of eighteen Dominic went to Confession to one of the Passionists. The priest asked him if he made mental prayer, and finding out that he did not, told Dominic to go and kneel in great recollection before God, and beg God to teach him mental prayer. Dominic's prayer was obviously heard, for he spent the next hour and a half in great devotion. The next time he went to Confession, the Passionist asked if he had followed the advice. Dominic said he had, and asked for further instruction. When the Confessor heard the length of time Dominic had remained in recollection, he knew that God must have helped him, and so he simply suggested that he go back to God for further instruction!

Dominic came directly into contact with the Passionist Fathers in 1810 when he was 18. He made a favourable impression on the Passionists, and one of them gave him lessons in Italian and French. Soon he was translating the French decrees promulgated by the French invaders - this following Napoleon's invasion of Rome in 1808. It was around this time he was introduced to a quarter of an hour's mental prayer each day and rapidly made progress. He wrote: "Before going to bed I have always found this time most helpful for this exercise - I recommend myself to the Madonna and beg for her help. Then I set about making my mental prayer. I received such downpours of grace that I was astonished... I was so changed that I seemed a different man."

Dominic says that as a result of his prayer he was given to understand that he could not save his soul by remaining in the world, and that it is impossible to continue meditation on the Passion and persevere in committing deliberate mortal sin. Unfortunately this fervour did not continue, and it was a serious illness and danger of death which brought him back to his senses. He recovered gradually over several months, and came to recognise the illness as a visit from God for which he was grateful. The spirit of thanksgiving always remained an outstanding characteristic of his spirituality.

Answering God's Call

Having overcome the crises of a possible marriage, and the risk of being enlisted in Napoleon's army, Dominic finally persuaded his uncle that his vocation was with the Passionists. Despite the uncle's love, and his hope that one day Dominic would inherit the farm, it was agreed that Dominic could present himself to the Passionists. However, there was a problem, namely that Religious Orders were still suppressed, and so Dominic was forced to wait a few years.

Religious vocation

These years were not barren for Dominic; they were filled with a series of temptations and consolations. He recognised three groups of temptations: the love of earthly goods, which he quickly subdued; concupiscence of the flesh, and pride of life - these latter two would disturb him throughout his life. The consolations came in the shape of both visions and voices, but like so many of the mystics, Dominic found it impossible to describe them. From his writings it would appear that most of these "revelations" came in the form of the spoken word. As the re-establishment of the Religious Orders seemed unlikely, he thought of joining a local group of hermits organised by a Frenchman. By way of preparing to make a final decision he made a novena at Pentecost and then went to Confession to the Passionist Provincial (the senior Religious in charge of a group of Retreats), who told him without hesitation he was to be a Passionist Brother, and promised to receive him as soon as the Order was re-established.

A lay brother

Following the disastrous attempt in 1812 to invade Moscow, Napoleon was severely weakened, and by 1813 the persecution of the Church abated, the suppression of the Religious Orders ceased, the Pope returned to Rome and the Passionists went back to their Retreat of Sant Angelo in Vetralla. Dominic moved in as a lay postulant i.e. someone who was going to live out their vocation as a Brother rather than as a Priest. He spent his time in manual work around the chapel and in the fields, but all the time he developed his relationship with God. His visions and voices were mainly about the attributes of God: His justice, His mercy, the mysterious ways of Divine Providence, and above all, the supreme lovableness of God. Central to his future development was the fact that in his prayer Dominic came to understand that sharing in the Passion of Christ is the safest way to sanctity.

Writing of this period he said: "I could never imagine that God designed me to do anything for his glory. My whole desire at the time was that God would design to furnish his Church with good pastors... Towards the end of that year [1813] on some evening of the Christmas festival, I was on my knees before God in my poor little room, beseeching him to provide for the necessities of his Church, when I heard an interior voice in set words, which did not leave a shadow of doubt as to its being from God. The voice told me that I was destined to announce the Gospel truths, and bring stray sheep back to the way of salvation. It did not specify to me how, or when, or to whom - whether infidels, heretics or bad Catholics - but left a hazy notion in my mind that the mission in store for me in future would not be among Catholics only."

This revelation caused Dominic to re-consider his position as a lay Brother. However, it was not within the Passionist tradition to allow someone to change their course of studies so as to become a priest. Both the Fr General (the head of the Order), and the Fr Provincial were fiercely opposed to any relaxation of this rule. Dominic never worried too much about such obstacles. He recalled that when he first went to Vetralla more postulants arrived than was expected, with the result that he had to sleep in the outhouse. He commented to the Novice Master "You will have room enough for me tomorrow night!" Sure enough, by the following night one of the postulants had left.

In his prayer he tried to discern where he was to be sent. He considered China and America, and gradually realised he would not remain a lay Brother, but would study and after six years "I was not to labour either in China or America, but in the north-west of Europe, and especially in England." After another revelation Dominic recorded "The name that remained most impressed on my mind was 'England', about which I did know something." The strange thing about this revelation is that it took place at the same altar where Paul of the Cross had his vision of Passionists working in England. Why either of these two men should have been devoted to England defies all explanation.

Road to priesthood

Dominic set off from Vetralla to the Novitiate House near Paliano, about sixty miles to the south of Rome, stopping one night in the Passionist mother house of SS John and Paul beside the Colosseum in Rome. He was received into the Novitiate as a lay Brother. Gradually the Novice Master took a close interest in Dominic as he recognised his intelligence. The Master was impressed not only by his familiarity with the Scriptures, but also Dominic's ability to translate and interpret them. The question of admitting Dominic as a clerical student was raised with the Fr General in Rome, who said he should be tested in Latin. The Novice master asked Dominic to translate the First Psalm into Italian and commented on how the work was done in less than quarter of an hour and far better than the Master could have done it. The General said it would be up to the local community to decide - they were unanimous in their vote to accept him as a cleric. He was clothed in the Passionist habit on 14th November 1814 at the age of twenty-two, and was given his Religious name of Dominic of the Mother of God.

Dominic was fortunate to have a highly experienced and holy Novice Master, Fr Bernard. He quickly realised that Dominic was well developed in the life of prayer, and had enjoyed great spiritual gifts from God. The time of the Novitiate is a time for both testing and teaching, and Fr Bernard set out from the beginning to do both. Years later Dominic commented that his novitiate year had been hard, but he was convinced that his Novice Master loved him despite the hardship and humiliation he imposed on him.

The Assistant Master was Fr Anthony who taught Dominic grammar and Latin. Dominic was so quick at learning that within two months he had overtaken the other clerical students in their study. Fr Anthony went on to become the General of the Congregation and it was he who eventually sent Dominic to England. Dominic described him as his "guide, philosopher and friend."

Student life

On 15th November 1815, Dominic took his vows of Poverty, Chastity, Obedience, and the fourth distinctive vow of the Passionists to promote devotion to the Passion of Jesus. Before moving on to the student house, Fr Anthony taught Dominic the basics of logic, and later reported that Dominic "made such progress in that short time that he could easily have taught the subject to his fellow students."

Initially Dominic was sent to Monte Argentaro, the first monastery founded by Paul of the Cross, about 80 miles north of Rome, on a promontory of land jutting out into the Mediterranean. After one year he was sent to the student house of SS John and Paul, and here Dominic spent his time with fifteen other students. He proved to have a quick and tenacious memory, and was able to recall material he had read years before as if he had read it yesterday. He had a keen thirst for knowledge and showed he had exceptional powers of concentration.

But life was not all study and books; Dominic had to take part in activities working in the garden, cleaning the house, and looking after any of the sick Religious. As the daily round of study and work developed, so too did Dominic's prayer life. He had never revealed how he had been favoured by God, and continued to experience visions and voices. It is important to realise that this did not result in some sort of dour and withdrawn character, but rather he was noted for his good humour and ability to radiate happiness. He was always prepared to join in with jokes.

One element of Dominic's prayer life at this time is his great devotion to the saints, not as a general group but as individuals. Thus he would set aside a day for each saint and pray to them for a particular grace; naturally one of the regular saints to be invoked was St Gregory for the conversion of England. Concern about England continued to obsess his thoughts and prayers, but he could not see how he would end up working there - he trusted in God, and had to wait.

Ordination

On account of his age Dominic's ordination was advanced on condition that he continued his studies afterwards. On 1st March 1818 Dominic was ordained in Rome. At this time he wrote an essay called a *Dialogue between a Young Priest and the Blessed Virgin*. In it Dominic protests that he is not worthy to touch the Body of Christ. Our Lady replies that he should deal with her Son as she had done from Bethlehem to Calvary: "Imagine that you are receiving him as I received him in my breast when he was incarnate, or as I welcomed him in my arms when he was born, and embraced him on the road to Calvary; or again as I received him when they took him down from the Cross... Think too, as you say Mass, that your office is not only to offer the Sacrifice but to pray for all Christian people, for Holy Church, for the conversion of sinners, and the salvation of all those souls whom God assigns to your care as children to their father." Dominic replies that he will do this to the very best of his powers.

His Calvary

After ordination he continued to receive many blessings, but he realised that God would ask great things of him - he said he was prepared to give all that was asked for. In June 1820 Dominic records that God asked him to agree to God's withdrawal from his life. In other words there were to be no more visions and consolations, but only the sense of absence of God as Jesus experienced on Calvary. Crucially he realised that this was not an invitation into the Dark Night, which is of restricted duration, but it was to be life-long. In the Christian tradition the Dark Night of the Soul, is part of a mystical process in prayer whereby individual souls are led to leave all knowledge and trust totally in the guidance of God; the Carmelite St John of the Cross was the great writer on this. To ensure Dominic had understood what God had said, he asked "Do you mean my God, that I shall have to endure for ever the awful agony that prostrates my heart now?" The silence implied that was precisely what was meant.

Dominic replied "Lord if it be possible, let this chalice pass from me; yet not my will, but thine be done."

Longing for England

He still had what he called "Visits" from time to time, but these brief episodes of consolation always warned him that greater trials were to come. However, he did not lose sight of England and wrote: "No matter how great my aridity may be, I will never cease to pray for the salvation of my brethren, and I protest that I will never cease praying for this intention until I see God's name known and honoured through the world, and especially until I see England reunited to the Church." A few months later he wrote: "I have experienced a great longing for the conversion of unbelievers, especially of England, and I have offered myself to God to be annihilated if annihilation could serve this purpose... if you [God] wish to condemn me to suffer all the pains that the English would have to suffer if they were damned I am content, provided only that they all return to you."

There can be no doubt that that momentous sacrifice was a central event in Dominic's life - a focal point of his ministry and the climax of his calls at Merlano and Sant Angelo. In imitation of Jesus, he was to contribute to the world's redemption, not primarily by preaching but by suffering and mystical death. His subsequent success as a missioner was not the principal purpose nor the major fruit of his vocation. Unless this is understood, his unique vocation might be dismissed as much ado about very little. No wonder one of his favourite and most frequently quoted texts was "Unless the grain of wheat dies, it remains alone."

Teacher

Following his agreeing to sacrifice any consolation from God, Dominic found himself struggling with prayer. He seems to have lost the grace of being aware of the presence of God and was reduced at times to simply trying to pray the Our Father. Strangely he never found any difficulty in praying to Mary and always was able to maintain with her an easy mother/son relationship at any time.

Dominic was 26 when he was ordained, but he was only half way through his course of studies; nevertheless by 1821 when he was 29 years of age, he was moved back to Sant Angelo at Vetralla as Professor of Scholastic Philosophy. This meant not only giving lessons to the students, but he was also responsible for their spiritual and temporal needs. Given his workload a number of his fellow priests were convinced that Dominic's knowledge had been given directly to him by God. He applied himself not only to his duties teaching, guiding and supporting the students, but also in shaping himself to conform to the Crucified Christ.

His lectures were never simply based on whatever text book the students were using. He constantly worked from the *Summa* of St Thomas Aquinas, and used the great books of theologians who had stood the test of time. Continuing his own personal quest for knowledge he perfected his study of Latin and went on to teach himself Greek, French and the rudiments of English. His French must have been more than adequate, for within a month of his arrival in Belgium he was able to preach a retreat in French. The reason he learned Greek was again with a view to the English mission. He had heard that many of the Anglican clergy were classical scholars, and so he concluded that Greek might be useful in debating with them. Subsequently on more than one occasion he did use Greek in his discussions with them. Dominic had little trouble in reading English, but as we saw at the very beginning of this story, he had major problems with the pronunciation.

Scripture was Dominic's first love and always remained his favourite subject. As a student he resolved that when he was able he would spend at least half an hour each day reading the Scriptures. He also said that his favourite authors were those whose name began with an 'S', that is, saints.

Pastor

On a pastoral level Dominic was constantly preaching in the church of the Retreat. While he was not noted as an orator, not least because he had quite a squeaky and weak voice, he had the eloquence of tremendous sincerity - and the local peasants recognised and preferred this to any flowery sermon. He enjoyed telling the story of how a peasant asked him one day: "Who preached last Sunday?" "Why do you ask?" replied Dominic. "Well whoever he was," answered the peasant, "he was a poor hand at it anyway." Dominic was intrigued and asked "What makes you think so?" The man replied "Just imagine even I could follow every word he said. He must be a very poor scholar if he could talk for an hour without using a single word not too big for a brain like mine." Unfortunately Dominic's reply is not recorded.

People thronged to him in the Confessional and he developed a full apostolate directing souls, not only from within the Passionist community, but from the surrounding area. In his "spare time" Dominic started to write on a wide range of topics: sermons for Sunday Masses and for Missions; a series of meditations on the Passion; a series of spiritual letters; instructions for those thinking of entering Religious Life; and a treatise on Mary. The archives of SS John and Paul contain over 100 volumes of Dominic's writings; sadly there is evidence that quite a few writings are missing. Nevertheless, it is clear he kept his vow of never wasting a moment of his life.

Theology

At the beginning of 1825 he was moved back to Rome to teach theology. At the end of his class he always asked his students to offer three Hail Marys for England. Rarely did a lesson pass without the students hearing something about England, and they quickly learned that if they wished to divert Dominic from a tricky issue, all they had to do was raise a question about England.

While teaching theology, Dominic had been told to write a course of philosophy by Fr General, and then to go to the Retreat at Ceccano, fifty miles south of Rome, and teach it to the students. But a crisis developed when the General accused Dominic of not remaining true to the teachings of St Thomas Aquinas. Dominic went and prayed at the feet of Our Lady, wrote a letter to the General who subsequently investigated the original claim, and declared the work to be sound.

Dominic's workload was phenomenal, and it is hard to see how he achieved so much so well. It is a fact that he slept very little and would rise at 2.30 for two hours study, then half an hour's preparation for Mass which he celebrated at 5.00 a.m. Soon after 6.00 he was back at his desk, and from then until noon engaged in study and teaching. In the afternoon he followed a similar programme of prayer and study. However, in a letter to a young priest just starting out on a teaching career he wrote "Do not take me as a model, I overdid things by depriving myself of necessary sleep."

Despite his heavy schedule of lectures, Dominic still found time to preach retreats during the holidays. On one occasion he was asked to give the community retreat the day before it was due to begin. This was no problem for Dominic, although most other men would have refused to take on such a task without at least a month or two to prepare. In both his preaching and giving retreats Dominic insisted that it was the message, and not the preacher, who should absorb the attention of the congregation. Unlike most of his contemporary preachers, Dominic's style was always homely and simple; the clergy commented that he gave more help to the theologian than to the public orator!

A great deal is known of Dominic's spiritual life because he was instructed by his spiritual director to write his autobiography. His whole attitude is evident in the title: *Outline of the Divine Mercy in the Conversion of a Sinner*. At first he was anxious about such a work as he feared he could be the victim of pride - he wrote it because he felt it was wrong to keep to himself his own reassuring story of God's mercy and the Madonna's protection.

Darkness

This period of Dominic's life is spectacular not only for the amount of work he got through, but also for the tremendous darkness he experienced in his life. Constantly he tried to pray "Do with me what you will." This prayer was accepted to the point that Dominic experienced a state known to some of the great saints as "mystical death." In a sense this experience should not surprise us, for it was the hallmark of the spirituality of St Paul of the Cross. At its heart is the reality of the soul being afflicted by all forms of deprivation, crushing sadness, the Agony in the Garden and the sweating of blood. Dominic said that at times it was worse than the power of hell.

Fortunately at this time Dominic had Fr Lawrence as his spiritual director. The wise and gentle priest taught Dominic the importance and necessity of patience with self. He showed him that it was not always prudent to go crashing in and attacking a weakness in oneself; consequently Lawrence was able to guide and support Dominic through showing that sometimes it was better to concentrate on developing the good rather than attacking the bad.

English contacts

Around 1829 Dominic was moved back to Rome to teach theology, and it was while he was in SS John and Paul that he began to develop contacts with English Catholics. The Second Spring - a title of a sermon by John Henry Newman - was beginning to emerge in England, but as yet Italy did not know this phrase which was to refer to the flowering of the Catholic Church again. The Second Spring is a concept which is applied to the Catholic Church in England, and spans the period from 1818 when the English College in Rome was reopened (this was a seminary to prepare men for the priesthood and to work in England), through to 1852 when the English Bishops met in synod for the first time after the restoration of the Hierarchy. It is a period filled with Italian missionaries moving into England e.g. Passionists, Redemptorists and Rosminians, while at the same time the numbers of Catholics increased hugely due to Irish immigration. Prior to 1850 the Church in England was divided into Districts administered by Vicar Apostolics, who were Bishops, and were directly responsible to Propaganda Fide in Rome as England was classed as a mission; but after the restoration Dioceses were created.

All Dominic could do in his isolated Retreat was to offer himself to God for England; he did manage to get the novices and their community to form a Holy League dedicated to prayer and penance for England's conversion; he had to wait for God's own time - a torture for a man so eager to get to England.

Courageous debater

Closer to home another storm was brewing. Fr Félicité de Lamennais was recognised as a genius due to the many books he wrote. A French political and religious writer, he was celebrated as the latest Father of the Church, and there was even talk of his being made a Cardinal. Everyone was praising him apart from two: John Henry

Newman, the Vicar of St Mary the Virgin, Oxford; and Dominic Barberi. Dominic had studied De Lamennais closely and had even written a pamphlet analysing his thoughts. Dominic had detected the spirit of pride and even unbelief; he said that the cynicism of De Lamennais ultimately led to unbelief. De Lamennais maintained that the individual is dependent on the community for his knowledge of the truth, and to isolate oneself is to doubt, effectively he opposed most traditional Catholic doctrines, but his eloquence gained him many fervent disciples.

Dominic basically said that the greatest Catholic writer of the day was in the wrong! He claimed that De Lamennais's principles would produce conclusions pernicious to both the Church and to society, and eventually laid the groundwork for Modernism which was later condemned by the Popes. Dominic was publicly reprimanded and humiliated, but fortunately he was not asked to withdraw his comments. In June 1833 the Pope condemned De Lamennais, and Dominic received a letter from the General stating that Dominic's analysis had been correct and everyone else was wrong! De Lamennais eventually left the Church and entered politics.

In Rome in 1830 Nicholas Wiseman was the Rector of the English College, the *Venerabile*. The *Venerabile* was a focal point for the Catholic English aristocracy who flocked to Rome while making the Grand Tour of Europe. One of Wiseman's students was the recent convert the

Honourable George Spencer (cf. CTS Saints of the Isles B 681). Spencer became a good friend of Wiseman's but was not afraid to urge him to "apply his mind to something more practical than Syrian manuscripts or treatises on geology, and instead to take up the English mission." Ten years later Wiseman became the president of Oscott College, and when the English Hierarchy was restored in 1850, he became the first Archbishop of Westminster.

George Spencer

Dominic had been asked to help Sir Harry Trelawney, a convert in his seventies, to learn to celebrate Mass. George Spencer was asked to act as translator, and with Ambrose Phillipps accompanied Sir Harry to the Passionist mother-house. Many years later Dominic wrote of this crucial meeting: "and these gentlemen gave me the first inkling of hope that perchance, in course of time, it might be arranged that I should go to England." Both Spencer and Phillipps were amazed when they discovered the intensity of Dominic's love for England. As we shall see, George Spencer became a close friend of Dominic and eventually made his profession of vows as a Passionist at the feet of Dominic.

Dominic trained the lay Brother in Rome who dealt with visitors to the Retreat of SS John and Paul, to ascertain from English visitors if they were Christian and Catholic. It was done in the form of a catechism question and answer session. The poor Brother, without understanding any English, then read a definition of what it meant to be a Catholic! If the visitor showed any sign of interest in becoming a Catholic, Dominic was to be sent for. The story was told of a Scottish gentleman who had been highly amused by the Brother's comic-opera English and unimpressed by his theology, but the broken words kept ringing in his ears. A year later he returned to announce that he and all his companions had become Catholics.

Dominic was now extremely happy for he had a direct link with his beloved England - how accurate and realistic the information he was given by Spencer and Phillipps, about the prospects of the Church in England, is clearly open to dispute. Certainly he had been led to believe that England as a nation was on the cusp of converting back to Catholicism. Dominic had no way to verify such a claim, but naturally believed two well-educated and devout Englishmen. All the time he was with them, Dominic tried to master the English language. Of course there was no mention at this time of the Passionists moving to England.

The Road to England

Just after he had got to know English people, just as he was beginning to develop his knowledge of the language, just when he was perfectly happy in Rome, Dominic was appointed Superior of the new Passionist Retreat at Lucca near Pisa, and he left Rome for ever in the summer of 1831. He was soon respected and loved both inside and outside of the community, and was also appointed as an advisor to the Provincial. However, this was a time of trials, as he was cut off from his English contacts, from his friends in Rome, and he suffered from the first of five hernias he was to have in his life, as well as recurring bouts of fever.

In addition to establishing the new community, Dominic continued his lecturing, and as his reputation for wisdom and holiness grew, he spent more and more time helping priests who came to him for advice. At the same time he would go into the students in the evening and read them extracts from letters about England; his own letters back to English contacts read like love letters! He was waiting for God to send him to England.

Preaching

On missions, aware of his limitations as a preacher because of his poor voice, he much preferred to spend his time giving instructions in the faith or hearing Confessions. But increasingly his time was being taken up by preaching retreats, especially to the clergy and young men preparing for the priesthood. Throughout this time Dominic was writing to, and receiving letters from, Spencer and Phillipps. Dominic's letters are filled with expressions of his longing to hear more about the progress of the Church in England, and all the time he expresses the hope that he may be able to go and work there - but in God's own time.

In May 1832 George Spencer was ordained a priest. This followed a severe attack of consumption, and when Dominic heard of it he invited Spencer to come to Lucca to convalesce. As things transpired, Spencer was able to spend only a few days (not the months both had hoped) with Dominic before returning to England.

In April 1833 the General Chapter of the Passionist Congregation took place. This is the supreme legislative assembly of the Order. Dominic attended the meeting and made a strenuous appeal for the Passionists to establish a community in England. He supported his argument by ranging from the vision of Paul of the Cross, to presenting a large file of supporting letters. He failed miserably! - crucially the project was not rejected but postponed until the next General Chapter in 1839, in another six years. Yet more waiting!

Appointed Provincial

Dominic was relatively fit at this time, the number of converts in England was growing following the passing of the Catholic Emancipation Act in 1829, and an increasing number of chapels were being built. All seemed ripe for Dominic, but still he had to wait. While waiting he was shocked to be told that he had been appointed Provincial, or major superior, of a number of communities, including the one he had first joined as a postulant. The priest who put Dominic in the outhouse on that first night must have had quite a surprise to meet him now as his Provincial!

As a major superior he insisted on the exact observance of the Rule; but he was always ready to dispense individuals from any particular mortification if there was just cause. Throughout this time his humility and personal holiness were models for all to follow. He took an active part in training and guiding the young missioners, and offered suggestions as to how they could improve.

Health

Dominic's health became a major, while hidden, issue. As a student he developed a hernia which steadily got worse; he suffered rheumatism and palpitations of the heart; he frequently suffered inflammation of the chest, and at times describes spitting blood, leading to the conclusion that he, like George Spencer and Nicholas Wiseman, suffered from consumption or TB. Despite all his health problems, and these were so severe as to provoke his being given the Last Rites at least twice, he often said "I shall die in England, and not anywhere else." The Last Rites were only given to people who were believed to be on the point of death.

Coincidentally, in 1834, both Dominic and Newman, who was in Sicily, were gravely ill. Both were confident that they would not die; Newman because he "had not sinned against the light"; and Dominic because the prediction of his voices had not yet been fulfilled. After Newman's recovery, while on his way back to England, he wrote *Lead kindly Light*.

Several stories are told of Dominic at this time surviving various dangers, including his falling in a swollen river and almost drowning under his horse. After instantly praying to Our Lady he found himself standing on the side of the river perfectly safe. In a similar way stories are told of his having the gift of bi-location or the ability to appear in two places at the same time. All sorts of extraordinary gifts were showered on Dominic at this time; he was able to prophesy, receive revelations and ecstasies, and could read a person's soul. He was gifted with several visions of Our Lady, and it was noticed that when he preached about her he often went into ecstasy - much to the alarm of his listeners, and his penitents in the Confessional.

Frustrations

In 1836 Dominic ceased being Provincial, but acted as the advisor to the new Provincial. Increasingly he was used by Bishops to bring about reconciliation in areas of conflict in their dioceses; but he never lost sight of his guiding principles. Thus when the Fr General asked him to preach a sermon in a particular style on one saint, he refused saying he was no good at such sermons. The General insisted, Dominic eventually complied, and the congregation was upset not to be treated to a flowery oratorical sermon, but rather an instruction on how they should their lives. Dominic was never asked to give such sermons again!

In 1837 Italy was swept by cholera. The heart of the disease was Ceprano, half way between Rome and Naples, and Dominic immediately set off to work with the sick and dying who had been isolated from the rest of the town - his "luggage" consisted of his Bible, breviary, and writing materials. At first he met hostility from both the local clergy and the few remaining doctors. Gradually as they saw his total dedication to the sick, the locals came to accept, then admire, and finally love Dominic. Many stories of miracles are told of this period, but possibly the most difficult one to understand is how Dominic found time to continue his writing.

In addition to all his administrative and preaching duties, Dominic would spend hours hearing Confessions.

People flocked to him for help and guidance even if it meant keeping him there until after midnight.

Desire for England

Dominic's passion for England continued, and he was delighted to hear of Phillipps establishing the Cistercians at Mount St Bernard in Leicestershire in 1835 - 300 converts were made in the parish in the first year of its founding. He saw this as a sign that it would not be too long before the Passionists had a community in his beloved country. All the news Dominic received suggested a revival of the Church in England had begun: Wiseman had returned to London; The Oxford Movement in the Anglican Church had established itself through the publication of Tracts or essays setting out their views, and particularly the writings of Newman; converts were flocking to the Church, including men like Augustus Pugin the architect who was to have such a huge influence on English church buildings. Pugin went on to design the interior of the House of Lords and many churches. Inevitably such progress provoked much hostility, especially from Protestant clergymen. At the same time Dominic was left feeling isolated as sometimes letters went astray, and at one point he went three years without receiving any letters from England - certainly a trying separation.

Phillipps eventually wrote to Dominic and offered to finance the Passionists once they arrived in England. Dominic wrote a letter accepting the offer, but first he submitted the letter to Fr General who refused permission for it to be sent, not least because he believed Dominic's health was not strong enough, but also because he felt there would be no companions to go with him. Not all Passionists had the same desire for England as Dominic.

Prayer for unity

Fr George Spencer went with Phillipps to convalesce in France in 1838. While in Paris Spencer established a Crusade of Universal Prayer for the conversion of England. The Crusade in various forms spread over much of Europe and included Emperors, Archbishops and peasants, but the single greatest contribution was when George Spencer promoted the Crusade among the Irish: he told them that God would listen to their prayers as they were praying for their persecutors - the English. This was to prove to be central to the life and work of George Spencer until his death in 1864. Naturally Dominic was delighted to hear of prayers battering the gates of heaven for England.

Space does not allow the telling of the complex negotiations carried on between the Passionists in Rome, their various lay benefactors, and Bishops in France. It was believed that a Passionist community would have to be established first in France. Dominic was not involved in any of these discussions. Dominic's basic attitude was: if my Superiors let me go to England, God would sort out the rest! It all seemed so simple to Dominic if one simply trusted in God.

The Passionist General Chapter took place in Rome in April 1839. This did not mean a green light was to be given to a new foundation in England. One powerful objection, put forward by an English priest, was that no Englishman would join the Passionists as they were so strict. However, the General Chapter was presented with a petition to establish the Passionists in England, based on the vision of Paul of the Cross. A house was offered by Phillipps, and funding was to be provided by a benefactor. The petition was adopted by a large majority and things looked bright for Dominic.

Further delays

Then disaster struck - Dominic was elected Provincial for the second time! He would be stuck in Italy for at least another three years; all he could do was dream. A mystery now arises, for the missioners chosen for England were never sent - this failure has never been satisfactorily explained. Suffice it to say that a decision was made to erect a Passionist foundation at Ère in Belgium.

Belgium was the stepping stone to England, and Dominic longed to go there, but his name was not on the list of missioners commissioned to head to the northern climate. Famously Dominic said to a fellow priest "You will see I shall be sent. They have already nominated those who are to go to Belgium, but the thing is not well done. Without me they will not set out - I have to go with them." It would appear that Our Lady had promised Dominic he would go this time. Fr Anthony had been instructed to lead the missionary band, but he begged the General to dispense him from the task; that same night a letter was sent to Dominic instructing him to lead the group. After a wait of 26 years, with many trials and frustrations, he was to head north of the Alps.

The basic attitude of Dominic was "Here I am, send me...yet not my will, but thine be done." Dominic was now 48 years old; he was frail and his body was wracked with illness. His community admired his courage, but queried his prudence. His letters of this time suggest he was going to England; in reality he was going to Belgium. On 26th May 1840, having received the blessing of Pope Gregory XVI, Dominic and his three companions boarded the boat for Marseilles - it was the feast of Our Lady Help of Christians.

Northwards

Within two months of arriving in Belgium, the first of the missionary band died; no doubt malnutrition played a part. The Passionists had not been made welcome in

Belgium; they were treated with suspicion and false allegations were laid against them. Their house was totally lacking in furniture apart from a few straw mattresses; they had to borrow a chalice to say Mass, and suffered as they did not have a chapel in the house. The local Bishop did not trust them and made them sit an examination in theology. Half way through this exam the senior examiner, recognising the wisdom and sanctity of Dominic's answers, turned to the others and said "But it is Fr Dominic who should be in our place, and we in his!" The Bishop became a firm friend of the Passionists.

English visit

In September 1840 Bishop Wiseman wrote to Dominic inviting him to come and inspect a possible site for a new foundation at Aston in Staffordshire. Dominic arrived in Folkestone on Guy Fawkes, 5th November 1840 - England at last! Apart from Wiseman and Spencer making Dominic welcome, the trip was a cold, painful and disappointing one. Dominic was shocked to see so much anti-Popery - and amazed to see so little enthusiasm for the faith he came to proclaim. Even the priests in the seminary of Oscott College near Birmingham, thought Wiseman, Spencer and Dominic were unrealistic and even fanatical. A major problem on this visit was that the resident priest in Aston would not relinquish his position, and the local Bishop advised against even visiting the place. Dominic waited for three weeks in Oscott and then returned to Ère. There was nothing else to be done except wait.

The community at Ère gradually became more secure. Dominic started to give retreats to communities of Religious and seminarians. While his French was not perfect, all were able to understand. He realised that there was no point just sitting and waiting for things to happen, and so he spent his time directing souls. Fortunately, despite his many frustrations, he continued to receive "lights" about his future apostolate in England. He was bemused by the fact that while he was in Belgium he enjoyed relatively good health. One thing Dominic was concerned with was the formation of new Passionists; he did not want to turn them into Italians, but good Religious, and so he advocated that "We must adapt ourselves to the spirit of the nation."

In February 1841 Newman published his famous Tract 90, and the Oxford Movement reached a cross-roads. Newman proved that the Thirty-nine Articles of the Church of England were not opposed to the Decrees of the Council of Trent. Newman was forced out of Oxford University and retired to Littlemore. The subject matter became a huge topic of dispute, even in the national press, and it was in the pages of newspapers that Dominic first earned a reputation for his learning among the English, including many Anglican clergymen.

England at last

At the age of 50, and after 28 years of waiting, Dominic was finally able to move to Oscott College in October 1841 - he had one companion with him. The dream had become a reality. But four more months would pass before the Passionists could take over in Aston, so Dominic spent more time improving his English. The frustration of waiting must have been like a living martyrdom for a man as zealous and energetic as Dominic. He was crushed as he came to realise that he would not see England converted in his own lifetime.

At his first public Mass in Aston, in February 1842, people laughed at his accent and appearance - they had been primed by the previous hostile parish priest; he was upset but never showed any resentment. Gradually the holiness of the man removed all opposition and the people came to respect and love him. On Good Friday 1842 he received his first English convert. Recognising that there were more Catholics in Stone he soon hired a room in a pub to celebrate Mass there. Stone was staunchly Protestant and violently anti-Catholic. As Dominic walked through the village in his black habit and sandals, the locals, led by their Protestant clergy, unleashed a barrage of abuse against him, and continued to do so for weeks. Mud and stones were thrown at him - one left a permanent scar on his head. Dominic simply walked calmly through the rabble, ignoring the mockery. Crosses and difficulties were his daily companions.

Each Sunday Dominic went to Stone and would hear confessions until 10.00; public prayers followed for fifteen minutes, and then he would preach for three-quarters of an hour. Mass followed at 11.00, and then Vespers were said at 3.00; this was followed by catechism for both children and adults. At 6.00 Dominic gave a lecture exclusively for non-Catholics - sometime as many as five hundred people crammed into the room, and two hundred more listened outside.

Opposition

A Calvinist minister decided to start a course of 24 lectures to expose "Papist errors". He planned on starting just as Dominic finished his talk. In fact he became so extreme and vicious that people compared his style with Dominic's and so abandoned him. Eventually the minister retracted everything he had said against the Catholic religion.

New Religious came to join the community, but not all were suited, whether they came from Italy, England or Ireland. The community consisted of three priests, two students for the priesthood, and three lay-brothers. Dominic had to function as Superior, novice master, parish priest, fund raiser, as well as give lectures each day in philosophy and theology. At the heart of Passionist life are the lynchpins of solitude, silence and prayer; Dominic had to shape and develop his Religious while at the same time come to terms with the reality of the Catholic Church in England. Despite all of that, he contemplated opening another community in the summer of 1844. Surprisingly, he still had time to follow all the controversy surrounding the Oxford Movement, and considered publishing some of his writings in English.

Local opposition gradually died down, and Wiseman advised Dominic to build a school in Stone, which could be used as a church on Sundays. Augustus Pugin drew up the plans and the foundation stone was laid in July 1843. Nearly seven hundred people, mainly Protestant, attended the stone-laying. By this date fifty-five people had been received as converts, but Dominic saw this as hopelessly small. He was also puzzled at his success, given that he knew how poor his English was and how difficult it was for people to understand him.

At the same time Dominic received a letter from Fr General chiding him for not writing to Rome so often - Dominic's excuse was the cost of postage! The General was keen to know what was going on in the newly founded mission, for recently he had also sent four Passionists to Australia - their mission failed and was not renewed until English Passionists went out in 1887. The sense of poverty was not only spiritual, but well rooted in material deprivation. However, Dominic reminded some of his students who had cut back on their meagre food "I will pay the butcher and baker, but not the doctor."

Apostolic work

By 1843 Dominic began to give retreats; the first Passionist retreat to Religious in England was at the Convent of Mercy in Handsworth, Birmingham. The following year he gave fifteen retreats - this while he was still giving lectures to his students in philosophy and theology! He gave retreats in Oscott, Swynnerton, Heythrop, Radford, Colwich, Stoke, Handsworth, Cheadle and Wolverhampton. For an infirm man who needed two people to help him mount a horse, this workload and travelling was truly heroic.

Frequently, people who kept any record of his preaching, commented on his abundant wit, but also his shrewd judgement of complex situations. His piety and charm also reinforced his arguments. Dominic was noted for his ability to bring about reconciliation at all levels of society, be it in a family row, or a celebrated public battle in the Press, as happened between Lord John Shrewsbury and Archbishop McHale of Tuam - two fiery and assertive characters. The background to the dispute was common throughout this period: Daniel O'Connell was fighting for Catholic Emancipation in Ireland, but the English would grant it only on condition that they could veto the appointment of Irish Bishops - a solution acceptable to English Catholics, but not to the Irish; there was tension between the new converts and the old Catholic families of England (Bishop Baines of the Western District wrote a pastoral letter in 1840 severely criticising the new converts); and constantly there were clashes in matters of Church and State. Archbishop McHale was said to be a "demagogue" by his opponents, as he used vivid and uncompromising language; Lord Shrewsbury was far more refined, but nevertheless the two engaged in controversial battles in the press. Dominic wrote to these two and said it would be better if they spent their time and energy fighting the opponents of the Church - much to everyone's surprise they agreed and peace was restored.

In a letter to Rome in 1843 Dominic wrote "There is little unity among Protestants, but there is also little among Catholics, and this is a great evil." He was appalled at some of the abrasive comments from Catholic clerics - comments which did not foster a spirit of harmony. He also wrote that many Englishmen needed to be convinced, not that the Catholic Church is the true Church of God, but that Christ is God. This was all so different from what he had expected.

By 1844 Dominic had overcome most of the local opposition and was able to organise a procession for Corpus Christi. He wrote to the General that over a thousand people had attended, half of them Protestant! The following year over 5,000 attended the procession.

Missioner

In addition to his community and parish work, Dominic introduced to England in 1843 the idea of a parish mission; this was a period of two or three weeks in which as many houses would be visited and people encouraged to come to the mission services, there would be an intense series of preached sermons and the opportunity for reconciliation with the Church, mainly through the Sacrament of Confession.

He recognised his stammering while preaching was an obstacle, but totally trusted in God, which was just as well, given that his first mission in Staffordshire got off to a disastrous start; evidently he was so nervous at trying to make a good impression, he was unintelligible for most of what he said. However, at the end of the second day a big Irishman followed Dominic into the sacristy, knelt at his feet and said "Your Reverence, the whole sermon struck me all of a heap; I did not understand more than a few words of it, and I don't know what foreign language you were talking. But I saw you stretch out your arms, and your voice had something so kind in it, that I said to myself: that holy man won't scold me, and I'll make my confession to him." The mission was a great success.

Requests for missions flooded in, and it upset Dominic that he had to turn down so many - this was not going to help him fulfil his dream of preaching all over England. The missions took on the set pattern of preaching, hearing Confession (for about fifteen hours each day), and instructing non-Catholics. Dominic later commented that he had never come across such fervent people, but he felt that the most effective form of preaching was good example and wearing the Passionist habit and sandals in public.

Reputation for holiness

Over the next five years Dominic was relentless in preaching missions all over England, from Winchester to York and all points in between. Toward the end of his life he calculated he had preached 100 missions and retreats. On his missions he received an average of fourteen converts. Interestingly members of his community commented on how his stuttering almost disappeared when he was preaching.

His reputation for sanctity spread, so that people would travel thirty miles and book into hotels in order to hear Dominic preach. All of his preaching focussed on the Passion, and the love and goodness of God. He gave the same message to priests, Religious, ordinands and the laity.

By 1845 Dominic was so crippled by his hernias, constant pain in the head, rheumatism, palpitations, heart attacks, and inflammation of the lungs that caused him to suffer with many colds, he said people thought he was 80 years of age. But he always felt he was strong enough to continue his work if God willed it.

Newman

It is patently false to subscribe to the notion that John Henry Newman was received into the Catholic Church by Dominic Barberi, as just a happy coincidence of being in the right place at the right time. Dominic's intellectual ability had been shown when he refuted De Lamennais, at a time when intellectual Europe was paying him homage. His voluminous writings on philosophy and theology had established him as a profound thinker, and thus well able to understand the intellectual journey and difficulties of Newman. But crucially, Dominic was also a holy man.

John Henry Newman (1801-1890) was brought up in the Church of England as an Evangelical. In 1828 he became vicar of St Mary's, Oxford where he became intimately involved in the Oxford Movement. Over the following dozen years he published his sermons from St Mary's, and these had a profound influence on the religious life not only of Oxford, but of the whole country. The spirituality of the sermons was the result of a close study of the writings of the Fathers of the Early Church. Between 1833-1841 Newman wrote twenty-four Tracts, popular statements of his religious position. The central belief was that there was a *Via Media* or middle way. Essentially he said that the Church of England held an intermediate position, represented by the patristic tradition of the Early Church as against modern Roman Catholicism on the one hand, and modern Protestantism on the other.

In the famous *Tract 90* he advocated the interpretation of the Thirty-nine Articles of the Church of England in a sense which agreed more or less with the Council of Trent. This provoked a huge row and Newman was silenced by the University. He began to have doubts about the claims of the Anglican Church, and in 1841 he gave up his position in Oxford and moved to the village of Littlemore. Here he established a semi-monastic community, and during the next few years lived in retirement with a few friends. He resigned the living of St Mary's in Littlemore in 1843.

Visit to Newman

In June 1844 Dominic paid a brief visit to see Newman, who like the other Tractarians were demanding proof of the sanctity of the Church of Rome. The argument was that while the Church of England lacked the note of unity, the Church of Rome lacked the note of sanctity. Newman summed it up by writing "If they [the Catholics] want to convert England, let them go barefooted into our manufacturing towns - let them preach to the people like St Francis Xavier - let them be pelted and trampled on, and I will own that they do what we cannot. I will confess they are our betters far."

Dominic wrote that Newman and his community made him welcome - probably recognising Dominic's spiritual stature. Years later Newman wrote "When his form [Dominic's] came in sight, I was moved to the depths in the strangest way. His very look had about it something holy." Newman recognised sanctity when he met it; he knew Dominic to be an intellectual and a holy man.

Dominic arrived at Littlemore on his way to Belgium on 9th October 1845. He had travelled for twelve hours on the outside of a stagecoach in driving rain. As he tried to dry himself in front of the fire at Littlemore, Newman entered, knelt at his feet and asked to be received into the Catholic church. The next day two more Tractarians made their profession of faith with Newman. This was not some minor private event, it became THE talking point of England, it also provoked a surge of anti-popery.

Newman went to Rome where he was ordained, and then returned to Birmingham where he established the Oratorians. Subsequently he went to Dublin as the rector of the short-lived Catholic university from 1854-58, and then spent time writing, including *The Dream of Gerontius* and his *Apologia pro vita sua*. In 1879 he was created a Cardinal.

Passionist expansion

Dominic's activity was ceaseless. He worked to establish a new community at Woodchester in Gloucestershire, and on 25th March 1846 he said the first Mass there. Dominic would long to be free of parish work, but the Bishops had made it a rule that any Religious Order would be allowed to live in their areas only on condition that they ran a parish. Naturally Dominic set forth with enthusiasm preaching, instructing, reconciling, and converting. He was showered with invitations to establish new communities, and rejected ten offers in one year alone. The community at Woodchester was to become the house of studies, and so seven of the community from Aston moved down to join Dominic who once more started a course of lectures for them.

Before any monastery should be built, like Solomon Dominic insisted that a church should be built first. Engaged in lecturing, administration, and developing the Province, Dominic had less time for missions and retreats, fortunately others were emerging to help him. From Italy there was Fr Gaudentius Rossi and Fr Vincent Grotti, from Holland Fr (now Saint) Charles of Mount Argus in Dublin, and from England Fr George Spencer who took the Religious name of Ignatius (a great, great grand uncle of the late Princess Diana), and from Ireland the Duke of Wellington's nephew: Charles Pakenham who became known as Fr Paul Mary who went on to become the first Superior of the Passionist Retreat of Mount Argus in Dublin. Poverty was the hallmark of each of Dominic's foundations; his basic attitude was: if God wants it, he will provide. This does not mean he was unaware of bills etc., for he wrote to the General reporting that a number of people had remained in the Retreat several days and contributed nothing; similarly he had travelled to give missions and was not even given the money to cover his travel costs - small as they were.

Irish immigration

In 1845, and again in 1846, the potato crop failed in Ireland due to blight. This resulted in large scale emigration to both England and America, and in its turn created the foundation of the Church in these countries as we know it today. But it was only the relatively fit and wealthy who were able to escape; hundreds of thousands died of the famine. The area around Aston and Stone is known as the Potteries, and it was to these parts that thousands of starving Irish came - they brought their faith, but nothing else.

Dominic and his companions went to work among these people - Ignatius Spencer was required to go out and look after the sick and dying in the workhouse while still in the middle of his novitiate (a year in which one is not allowed outside of the community); this nearly killed him and he was given the last rites, but he survived and made his Profession on 6th January 1848. Despite their absolute poverty, the Community saved some money and sent it via the *Tablet* paper to the Bishop of Kerry to help relieve some of the suffering.

While the fever and famine eventually passed, the Irish remained and so required ministering to. A new church was required at Aston, and the foundation stone was laid in 1846, despite there being no funds. Dominic knew God would not let him down. His community suffered various forms of illness and Dominic had to struggle on with his own infirmities. He was tireless in preaching retreats, but kept a close eye on the building of the churches in Aston and Woodchester.

As Dominic ran the young Province he not only had to worry about the formation of novices and students, he also had to cope with a number of his young priests dying. A tension must have existed as he tried to deal with all these "domestic" issues, while trying to develop his own national apostolate: the conversion of England.

London mission

In August 1847 Nicholas Wiseman was appointed Bishop of the London District; he wrote to Dominic and asked him to establish a Passionist community in London. The following year they moved into Poplar House, Hampstead - an isolated house ideally suited as a base for working in London and the surrounding villages; the parish took in much of the Edgware Road, included Kilburn and reached as far north as Watford. Less than two years later the community moved to the Hyde near Hendon, before finally moving to St Joseph's, Highgate Hill in north London. One story told of Dominic at this time recalls how each morning a small milk-maid brought the milk; he looked critically at the fluid in the can and eventually said to her "My child, will you tell your mother to put a little more milk in the water the next time."

In January 1849 Dominic visited St Helens in Lancashire with Fr Ignatius and John Smith, a local wealthy contractor who wanted to donate land and build a church. After inspecting three sites Dominic made his decision and said "This is the place of my rest for ever. Here will I dwell because I have chosen it." The foundation stone at Sutton was laid on the day of Dominic's funeral in Stone, and eventually it was here that he was laid to rest.

As missions and retreats increased, so too did the number of converts - to receive forty into the Church after a mission was not unusual. Commenting on Dominic's style of giving missions, again and again people mention his spirit of gentleness and holiness. However, in March 1849 he developed a new idea as he preached a two week mission in Horseferry Road: clad in full Passionist habit and sandals, the missioners went out into the streets inviting the people to the mission, to

"Know Popery." This was a dangerous move and could be seen as provocative, but there is no record of any backlash. This broke the ice and established the precedent and example for the work of the Catholic Evidence Guild years later.

In the same mission Fr Ignatius Spencer preached an aggressive sermon on the conversion of England and was surprised to be criticised by Dominic. Ignatius suggested that Dominic was not as keen as he used to be on England's conversion. In his humility, Dominic agreed, but was obviously upset by the remark. The next morning Ignatius apologised, and while Dominic accepted the apology he said "Yes, yes, but not so much heat my dear; let us proceed peacefully."

The Passionists enjoyed a reputation for being good and holy Religious. In 1847 when talks were taking place to re-establish the Hierarchy (which happened in 1850), it was proposed that Dominic would be appointed Bishop of Reading, and Ignatius as Bishop of Bury St Edmunds. Many people were claiming that Dominic was a saint. Wiseman, Spencer, Faber, Newman and many others turned to him for advice.

Dublin mission

In April and May 1849, Dominic, Ignatius Spencer and Vincent Grotti conducted the first Passionist mission in Ireland at St Andrew's, Dublin. Each spent a minimum of twelve hours every day in the Confessional, and that was still not enough; some people waited from 5.00a.m. to 11.00p.m. The evening service often lasted two and a half hours! Fifteen Protestants were received into the Church (an extraordinary result in Ireland); and on the last day of the mission 3000 people received Communion.

Approaching the end

It would appear that Dominic had clear knowledge of his approaching death. Strangely despite all his labours and worries his health was better now than when he first arrived in England. In the middle of August 1849 Dominic made a visit to the community in Ère, returning by the end of the month. He planned to go to Woodchester for the opening of the new church, and Fr Louis, a distant relative, asked if he could accompany Dominic - he was refused because of the expense. Louis persisted, and the next morning Dominic relented.

Early the next morning Dominic celebrated Mass and he and Louis set off towards Paddington station. On the way Dominic said that the end of his life had now come. Having passed Reading in the train, Dominic experienced a severe pain in the head which seems to have moved to his heart - he knew he was dying. The train stopped at Pangbourne and a doctor, who diagnosed a heart attack, helped lift Dominic into the home of a friendly Protestant. He was unable to sit and eventually lay down on straw and writhed in agony. The local inns would not accept Dominic as he had come from London where cholera was raging. The doctor decided to move him back to Reading by train; as they waited on the platform he made his Confession. In Reading the doctor and Fr Louis got Dominic into the "Railway Tavern", and put him to bed. The doctor thought he would survive; Dominic knew he would not.

Despite his severe pain he thought of the well-being of the Province, and instructed that Fr Ignatius should take over as Provincial; he then fell asleep. Five hours after the severe pain began Dominic died - it was about 3.00p.m on the 27th August 1849. He was fifty-seven years old; he had spent 34 years as a Passionist, and had worked in England for 8 years; and yet most of his adult life had been offered to God for England.

No announcement was made about his remains being taken to Stone, but as his body was carried down the streets where a few years earlier he had been insulted and assaulted, people came in their thousands to pay their respect. The Requiem Mass took place on 31st August. He was buried in the new church at Aston, but eventually was moved to Sutton, which he had declared would be his final resting place. In the church of St Anne and Blessed Dominic, his mortal remains lie beside Fr Ignatius Spencer and Mother Mary Joseph Prout, in what Archbishop Beck of Liverpool prophesied would be known as "The church of the three saints."

May They All Be One

The life of Dominic Barberi is well chronicled by both himself and his contemporaries. In essence it is a love story; a passionate love story for England. It began in Italy and after a long period of maturing it developed in Belgium and blossomed in England. It is not a romantic story as it is marked by suffering, deprivation, frustration and disappointment. Some may believe that it is a failure, just as Calvary appeared to be a failure. Dominic only worked in England for eight years, made relatively few converts, established three communities of his Order, gave a small number of missions and retreats, and crucially failed to see the conversion of England. So why should he be declared a saint? What is there in his life that is worthy of imitation?

Like Jesus of Nazareth, much of Dominic's life was hidden; only God knows, but it is probable he achieved far more for England in the trials and sufferings of his hidden life before he ever came to these islands. Like Jesus he died almost alone and in apparent failure. Like Jesus he constantly proclaimed the love of the Crucified God. Like Jesus he always acted in total charity, and even in his darkest hours never lost his trust and confidence in God. Like Jesus he had great love for Mary, and was always eager to have her interceding for him - and there is ample evidence that she listened to him.

Despite the visions, ecstasies, and lights, people were more impressed by his humanity than by his sanctity. Many people today would feel uncomfortable with the talk of visions and ecstasies, but that is not how people saw him, for that was part of his interior life in the Spirit. He was very much a man's man, not given to politics or scheming - for the simple reason he trusted totally in God being a very real and active presence in his life.

Dominic was certainly austere, but never forbidding. Holiness shone through, and so he was attractive to others; be it the great intellectuals of his day, or the smallest of children; be it members of his own community or people from other Christian denominations. His driving ambition for the unity of all Christians gave purpose and meaning to his pastoral work.

His humour was able to be put to good use, but never at the risk of hurting someone. The story was told that while he was in London a reputed visionary was sent to see him. Dominic welcomed her and listened to how she had had a vision of the Father and the Son. He said it was a great privilege, but was curious to know when this had happened. She said it was the previous day at 6.00p.m. He asked when did she dine, and she replied about 5.00, clearly annoyed at this irreverent form of questioning. She explained that she had consumed two glasses of port with the meal. Dominic said "Well my child, drink three glasses of port next time, and I promise that you will see the Holy Ghost as well."

Ultimately Dominic was a man of deep prayer. Yes, he had been blessed with many graces by God, but unlike most people who give up when the going gets tough, he not only persevered, but thanked God for his many crosses. He is a model of trust and perseverance, a man filled with a sense of patience as he waited to learn the will of God, and through it all, a sense of gratitude that God would have anything to do with him.

Dominic had spent most of his life praying, through the intercession of Mary, for England. When he arrived in his adopted country he believed he was fulfilling the vision of St Paul of the Cross. With Fr Ignatius Spencer he embarked on a huge mission to bring England back to "Unity in the Truth." These heroic men and their companions worked in an atmosphere of hostility, but they did not count the cost, for they believed it was all God's will. Their model was the Christ of the Passion, and they believed that it was not so much their preaching, but their example and above all their prayer that would bring about an answer to the prayer of Jesus: "That they may all be one."

The Passionists

The Passionist Congregation was founded in Italy in 1720 by St Paul of the Cross, and brought to England in 1842 by Blessed Dominic Barberi. It is a worldwide Order of priests and brothers who preach the love and suffering of the Crucified Christ.

Further information about Blessed Dominic Barberi, Fr Ignatius Spencer or Mother Mary Joseph Prout may be obtained from:

The Secretary, Sutton Shrine Trust,
St Anne and Blessed Dominic,
Monastery Lane,
Sutton,
St Helens,
Merseyside. WA9 4ZD

The Postulator

For information about favours received through the intercession of Blessed Dominic, please contact the Vice-Postulator:

Fr Ben Lodge, C.P.,
The Retreat,
3 Sea Street,
Herne Bay,
Kent. CT6 8SP

Informative Catholic Reading

We hope that you have enjoyed reading this booklet.

If you would like to find out more about CTS booklets - we'll send you our free information pack and catalogue.

Please send us your details:

Name ....

Address ....

....

....

Postcode ....

Telephone...

Email ....

Send to: CTS, 40-46 Harleyford Road,
            Vauxhall, London
            SE11 5AY

Tel: 020 7640 0042
Fax: 020 7640 0046
Email: info@cts-online.org.uk